CRIME CRIES CABALS

Finding Solutions to Africa's Worst Economic, Religious, and Socio-political Culture

Chris Leo

CRIME CRIES CABALS

By Chris Leo

July 2024
© Palace Media Publishing
palacemedia338@gmail.com

All Rights Reserved

CONTENTS

WEALTH AND POVERTY 34

SHADOWS OF TYRANNY 64

A CYCLE OF SQUANDERED OPPORTUNITIES 86

THE INTERPLAY OF FAITH AND POWER 103

THE SHADOWY NETWORKS OF POWER 109

VOICES IN THE MARGINS 115

THE POWER OF KNOWLEDGE 121

INTRODUCTION

Africa is the continent with the largest number of black people on this planet Earth. The continent makes up 10% of the world's population and 40% of the world's natural resources. Yet, it staggers at the precipice of poverty with an alarming rate of displaced persons scattered all over the world.

This book seeks to dissect the origin of these quagmires in the continent. It explores the causes and consequences of failed systems and processes, which are central to the woes of the continent. It takes the blame to the quarters responsible for the terrible woes. We will unravel the multifaceted nature of Africa's predicaments, exploring how criminal elements, powerful cabals, and systemic corruption have entrenched themselves within the fabric of society.

We will journey through the corridors of power, the bustling marketplaces, and the sacred spaces of worship to understand how these forces have influenced and often derailed the continent's path to development.

Each chapter weaves together narratives, data-driven analysis, and practical solutions to engage you and inspire action towards building a more prosperous and equitable Africa. The references reveal the depth of neglect and deliberate acts of maladministration by successive leaderships across the African continent.

However, this is not merely a catalogue of woes. ***"Crime Cries Cabals"*** is, at its core, a quest for solutions. By analyzing successful case studies, innovative approaches, and grassroots movements, my aim is to illuminate pathways toward meaningful change. From economic reforms and religious reconciliation to political restructuring and social empowerment, this book presents a comprehensive toolkit for addressing Africa's most pressing issues.

This book serves as a reminder of the fact that a people is responsible for the kind of environment they live in, and the kind of people that lead them. The solutions proffered in this book are sure tickets to getting the continent and her people out of the numerous problems created by the past and even present stakeholders.

Crime, Cries and Cabals make for a good research and history document from an intelligent and thinking mind who authored the book, Crime Cries Congressmen – addressing America's worst nightmares and violent gun culture. To a great and glorious Africa!

Rev. Chris Leo

CHAPTER 1

UNPACKING AFRICA'S HISTORICAL CONTEXT

ECHOES OF THE PAST

In the heart of Africa lies a narrative woven with threads of triumph and tragedy, resilience and oppression. To understand the complexities of its present, one must journey back through the annals of time, tracing the footprints of conquerors and the echoes of civilizations lost to the winds of change.

The Legacy of Colonialism

Africa's story is inseparable from the specter of colonialism that looms large over its history. From the scramble for Africa in the late 19th century to the imposition of arbitrary borders and exploitative economic systems, colonial powers left an indelible mark on the continent's destiny. The extractive industries established during this era laid the foundation for the exploitation of Africa's vast natural resources, while the divide-and-rule tactics sowed seeds of discord among its diverse peoples.

The Berlin Conference of 1884–1885, where European powers partitioned Africa among themselves without regard for indigenous boundaries or cultural identities was the beginning of Africa's woes. Unfortunately, the leaders of present-day Africa are still cooperating with that impish masterplan to the detriment of all Africans. The aftermath is the slavery mentality and over-dependence of African nations on the Western world.

Factors That Undermine Human Rights of Africans

The Berlin Conference of 1884-1885, also known as the Congo Conference or the West Africa Conference, was a meeting organized by the European powers to establish rules for the colonization and partition of Africa. While the conference aimed to resolve potential conflicts among the colonial powers, it had several negative consequences for the people of Africa and their human rights. Here are some factors that undermined Africa's human rights because of the Berlin Conference:

Disregard for African sovereignty

The conference divided African territories among European powers without any representation or consultation with African leaders or communities. This complete disregard for the sovereignty and self-determination of African peoples was a violation of their fundamental human rights.

Facilitation of colonial exploitation

The conference effectively legitimized and facilitated the scramble for Africa, paving the way for European colonial powers to establish control over vast territories and exploit their resources and labor. This exploitation of African peoples and resources was often accompanied by human rights abuses, such as forced labor, displacement, and violence.

Arbitrary Border Creation

The borders drawn by the European powers at the Berlin Conference often cut across existing ethnic, linguistic, and cultural boundaries, leading to the fragmentation of African communities and the subjugation of certain groups to foreign rule. This disregard for the identities and self-determination of African peoples was a violation of their human rights.

Promotion of European Economic Interests

The conference primarily served the economic interests of the European powers, with little regard for the well-being or rights of African populations. The focus was on securing access to resources, trade routes, and markets, rather than protecting the human rights of Africans.

Perpetuation of Racist Ideologies

The conference was underpinned by prevailing racist ideologies of the time, which viewed Africans as inferior and justified their subjugation and exploitation. This reinforced the dehumanization and denial of basic human rights to African peoples.

It is important to note that the Berlin Conference was a pivotal event that facilitated and legitimized the colonial subjugation of Africa, setting the stage for widespread human rights violations and the suppression of African self-determination for decades to come.

The Struggle for Independence

The mid-20th century witnessed a wave of fervent nationalism sweeping across Africa as colonized nations rose up against their oppressors in pursuit of self-determination. From Ghana's declaration of independence in 1957 to the liberation struggles in countries like Algeria, Kenya, and Zimbabwe, Africans fought valiantly to reclaim their sovereignty and chart their own course. Yet, the euphoria of independence was often short-lived, as newly formed nations grappled with the daunting task of nation building amid the wreckage of colonialism.

The Mau Mau Uprising in Kenya, where indigenous Kikuyu fighters resisted British colonial rule in the 1950s, highlighting the brutality of colonial repression, formed a pivot for subsequent quests for freedom.

This uprising was a significant armed resistance against British colonial rule in present-day Kenya. The Mau Mau movement, primarily consisting of members of the Kikuyu, Embu, and Meru ethnic groups, sought to reclaim their land and freedom from British colonial authorities. The uprising, marked by guerrilla tactics and brutal counterinsurgency measures by the British, lasted for nearly a decade before being suppressed. However, it played a crucial role in the eventual independence of Kenya in 1963.

Other uprisings in Africa that resisted colonialism before independence include:

Zulu Resistance (1879-1887)

A series of battles fought between the Zulu Kingdom and the British Empire in present-day South Africa.

The Zulu Resistance was a series of battles fought between the Zulu Kingdom and the British Empire in present-day South Africa. The Zulu people, led by King Cetshwayo, fiercely resisted the encroachment of British colonial forces into their territory. The conflict began in 1879 when the British invaded Zululand, leading to major battles like Isandlwana and Rorke's Drift. Despite initial victories, the technologically superior British forces eventually defeated the Zulu. This led to the destruction of the Zulu Kingdom.

Maji Maji Rebellion (1905-1907)

The Maji Maji Rebellion was an armed resistance against German colonial rule in present-day Tanzania. It was sparked by a cotton plantation policy imposed by the Germans, which led to widespread resentment among the indigenous population. The uprising, which took its name from a ritualistic belief in magic water (maji) that would protect fighters from German bullets, involved over 20 ethnic groups and was one of the largest rebellions against colonial rule in African history. Despite initial success, the superior German forces eventually crushed the rebellion.

Ashanti Wars (1824-1901)

The Ashanti Wars were a series of conflicts between the Ashanti Empire and the British Empire in present-day Ghana. The Ashanti, a powerful West African kingdom, resisted British attempts to expand their control over the region. The wars spanned several decades, with major battles like the Battle of Amoaful in 1824 and the Battle of Kumasi in 1874. The British eventually defeated the Ashanti and annexed their territory, leading to the establishment of the British Gold Coast colony.

Herero and Nama Genocide (1904-1908)

The Herero and Nama Genocide was an uprising against German colonial rule in present-day Namibia, which led to one of the earliest genocides of the 20th century. The Herero and Nama peoples, facing widespread land dispossession and oppressive policies, launched an armed resistance against the German colonial forces. The German response was brutal, with the implementation of extermination policies that led to the deaths of up to 80% of the Herero population and around 50% of the Nama population.

Algerian War of Independence (1954-1962)

The Algerian War of Independence was a protracted conflict between the Algerian National Liberation Front (FLN) and the French colonial forces. The FLN, seeking independence for Algeria, launched an armed struggle against French colonial rule in 1954. Guerilla tactics, urban warfare, marked the war and brutal counterinsurgency measures by the French. After years of fighting and international pressure, the French were forced to negotiate, leading to Algerian independence in 1962.

Mahdist War (1881-1899)

The Mahdist War was a religious and nationalist uprising against the British and Egyptian colonial rule in present-day Sudan. Muhammad Ahmad, a religious leader who proclaimed himself the Mahdi (the Guided One) and called for a jihad against the colonizers, led it. The Mahdist forces achieved several victories, including the capture of Khartoum in 1885, but were eventually defeated by a joint Anglo-Egyptian force in 1899.

Adwa Victory (1896)

The Adwa Victory was a decisive battle in which the Ethiopian Empire, led by Emperor Menelik II, defeated the Italian colonial forces in present-day Eritrea. The Italians, seeking to expand their colonial foothold in the region, invaded Ethiopia but the well-organized and motivated Ethiopian forces decisively defeated them at the Battle of Adwa in 1896. This victory preserved Ethiopia's independence and served as a major blow to the Italian colonial ambitions in Africa.

Chimurenga Wars (1896-1897 and 1966-1979)

The Chimurenga Wars were two major uprisings against British colonial rule in present-day Zimbabwe. The First Chimurenga (1896-1897) was a violent uprising by the Shona and Ndebele peoples against the British South Africa Company's occupation of their lands.

The Second Chimurenga (1966-1979), also known as the Rhodesian Bush War, was a prolonged guerrilla war fought by African nationalist groups like the Zimbabwe African National Union (ZANU) and the Zimbabwe African People's

Union (ZAPU) against the white minority government of Rhodesia. The Second Chimurenga eventually led to the independence of Zimbabwe in 1980.

Samori Ture's Resistance (1882-1898)

Samori Ture's Resistance was a prolonged resistance led by Samori Ture against French colonial expansion in present-day Guinea, Mali, and Côte d'Ivoire. Samori Ture, a skilled military leader, established a powerful empire in West Africa and fiercely resisted French attempts to subjugate his territory. His forces employed innovative tactics, including the use of cavalry and modern weapons, but the technologically superior French forces eventually defeated them after years of intense fighting.

These uprisings, while varying in scale, duration, and outcomes, were significant attempts by African peoples to resist and challenge the imposition of colonial rule on the continent.

The Post-Colonial Quagmire

With independence came the promise of a brighter future, yet for many African nations, the road ahead was fraught with challenges. The legacy of colonialism cast a long shadow, as newly independent states inherited artificial borders, fractured societies, and neocolonial economic structures. The rise of authoritarian regimes, fueled by Cold War rivalries, stifled democratic aspirations and entrenched systems of patronage and corruption.

A worthy reference is the reign of Mobutu Sese Seko in Zaire (now the Democratic Republic of Congo). This reign featured kleptocracy and human rights abuses, emblematic of post-colonial abuses and authoritarianism.

The challenges faced by African nations in the post-colonial era have been numerous and multifaceted, with many of these stemming from the legacy of colonialism. Here are some of the major challenges and instances of bad governance that can be seen as direct or indirect aftermaths of colonialism in Africa:

1. Ethnic Tensions and Conflicts

Colonial powers often arbitrarily drew borders without regard for ethnic and cultural boundaries, leading to conflicts between different ethnic groups within the same country. Examples include the Rwandan genocide, the Darfur conflict in Sudan, and the Biafra War in Nigeria.

2. Authoritarian Regimes and Lack of Democracy

Many post-colonial African leaders adopted authoritarian styles of governance, suppressing dissent and opposition. Examples include the regimes of Idi Amin in Uganda, Mobutu Sese Seko in Zaire (now Democratic Republic of Congo), and Robert Mugabe in Zimbabwe.

3. Economic Exploitation and Dependence

African economies were largely structured to serve the interests of colonial powers, leading to a continued dependence on the export of raw materials and the import of finished goods. This has hindered economic development and industrialization.

4. Corruption and Mismanagement

Some post-colonial leaders and their associates have been accused of embezzling public funds and mismanaging resources, contributing to economic stagnation and underdevelopment. Examples include the regimes of Sani Abacha in Nigeria and Hosni Mubarak in Egypt.

5. Environmental Degradation

The exploitation of natural resources by colonial powers and post-colonial governments has led to environmental damage, deforestation, and loss of biodiversity. This has been particularly problematic in regions like the Niger Delta in Nigeria.

6. Lack of Infrastructure

Many African nations inherited inadequate infrastructure from their colonial rulers, hindering economic development and the provision of basic services to citizens.

7. Brain Drain

The emigration of skilled professionals and intellectuals, often due to political instability or economic reasons, has deprived many African nations of valuable human capital.

8. Border Disputes

The artificial borders drawn by colonial powers have led to numerous territorial disputes between African nations, sometimes resulting in armed conflicts, such as the Eritrean-Ethiopian War.

9. Debt Crisis

Many African nations have struggled with high levels of external debt, often taken on during the post-colonial period, which has hindered economic growth and development efforts.

10. Dependency on Foreign Aid

The reliance of many African nations on foreign aid and assistance from international organizations and donor countries has sometimes led to a lack of self-sufficiency and sovereignty in policymaking.

It is important to note that while these challenges are significant, many African nations have also made progress in overcoming colonial legacies, with examples of successful democratic transitions, economic growth, and regional cooperation. However, the lasting effects of colonialism continue to shape the political, economic, and social landscapes of many African countries.

The Persistence of Structural Injustice

Despite strides towards political emancipation, Africa continues to grapple with the enduring legacies of its past. Structural injustices, from unequal distribution of wealth to entrenched systems of privilege and discrimination, perpetuate cycles of poverty and inequality. The scars of colonialism run deep, manifesting in the form of economic exploitation, cultural imperialism, and marginalization of the various geopolitical entities.

The legacy of apartheid in South Africa, a system of institutionalized racial segregation and discrimination is an example. The evil system that endured for nearly five decades left a legacy of economic disparities and social division.

The legacy of colonialism in Africa has manifested in the persistence of structural injustices that continue to hinder the development and progress of many nations on the continent. Here are some examples of these structural injustices and suggestions for global best practices to help overturn them:

1. Economic Exploitation and Dependency:

Many African economies remain heavily reliant on the export of raw materials and primary commodities, while importing finished goods, perpetuating a neo-colonial economic model. This has led to a lack of industrialization, limited economic diversification, and vulnerability to global market fluctuations.

Best practices: Encourage industrialization and value-addition to natural resources, promote economic diversification, and foster regional economic integration to create larger markets for African goods and services.

2. Land Dispossession and Inequality:

Colonial land policies often led to the dispossession of indigenous populations from their ancestral lands, creating a system of unequal land ownership and access. This has contributed to poverty, food insecurity, and conflicts over land rights.

Best practices: Implement land reform policies that address historical injustices, promote equitable land redistribution, and recognize customary land tenure systems.

3. Marginalization of Indigenous Communities

Many indigenous communities in Africa have faced marginalization, displacement, and exploitation of their traditional lands and resources, often in favor of extractive industries or commercial agriculture.

Best practices: Respect and protect the rights of indigenous communities, ensure their participation in decision-making processes that affect them, and promote the preservation of their cultural heritage and traditional knowledge.

4. Gender Inequality and Discrimination:

Colonial policies and practices often reinforced patriarchal systems and gender discrimination, limiting women's access to education, employment, and ownership of resources.

Best practices: Promote gender equality and women's empowerment through policies and programs that address gender-based violence, improve access to education and healthcare, and support women's economic and political participation.

5. Environmental Degradation and Resource Depletion:

The extractive and exploitative practices of colonial powers and subsequent governments have led to environmental degradation, deforestation, and the depletion of natural resources, disproportionately affecting marginalized communities.

Best practices: Adopt sustainable development practices, promote renewable energy sources, implement reforestation and conservation programs, and involve local communities in environmental decision-making processes.

6. Weak governance and institutions:

Colonial legacies have contributed to the persistence of weak governance structures, corruption, and lack of accountability in some African nations, hindering economic and social progress.

Best practices: Strengthen democratic institutions, promote transparency and anti-corruption measures, foster decentralization and local governance, and invest in capacity building for public institutions.

To overturn these structural injustices effectively, a combination of local, national, and global efforts is necessary. This includes policies and initiatives that address historical injustices, promote inclusive development, strengthen governance and institutions, and foster regional and international cooperation. Additionally, the active participation and empowerment of marginalized communities in decision-making processes are crucial for achieving sustainable and equitable outcomes.

Navigating the Shadows of History

As we stand at the crossroads of Africa's past and present, the echoes of history reverberate through the corridors of power and the corridors of our collective memory. To forge a path towards a brighter future, we must confront the ghosts of our past with courage and humility, acknowledging the wounds that bind us and the resilience that defines us. Only then can we begin to unravel the tangled skein of Africa's historical narrative, weaving a new tapestry of hope and possibility for generations yet to come.

CHAPTER 2

THE PARADOX OF
WEALTH AND POVERTY

WEALTH AND POVERTY

Africa should not only be known as the Black Continent but a continent of contradictions. Africa, a continent blessed with abundant natural resources, stands as a paradox of wealth and poverty. From the oil-rich plains of Nigeria to the diamond-studded soil of Botswana, the continent's riches are as vast as they are varied. Yet, amidst this cornucopia of resources, millions of Africans languish in the grip of poverty, their dreams deferred by the harsh realities of economic deprivation and social injustice.

The paradox of wealth and poverty in Africa is a striking and perplexing phenomenon that has persisted for decades, despite the continent's abundance of natural resources and economic potential. This paradox is characterized by the coexistence of immense natural wealth and widespread poverty, underdevelopment, political instability and economic stagnation.

Africa is endowed with a vast array of natural resources, including fertile lands, diverse minerals, and abundant energy sources. The continent holds vast reserves of oil, gas, gold, diamonds, copper, and other valuable minerals. Additionally, many African nations have rich agricultural potential, with fertile soils and favorable climatic conditions for various crops.

Despite this wealth of resources, a significant portion of Africa's population lives in extreme poverty, with limited access to necessities such as clean water, healthcare, education, and adequate housing. According to the World Bank, over 40% of the population in Sub-Saharan Africa lived on less than $1.90 per day in 2019, a widely accepted measure of extreme poverty.

We can attribute this paradox to a complex interplay of historical, political, economic, and social factors that have hindered the effective utilization and equitable distribution of Africa's resources.

Factors Behind the Paradox

1. Colonial Legacy And Resource Exploitation

The legacy of colonialism has played a significant role in shaping the paradox of wealth and poverty in Africa. During the colonial era, African resources were exploited for the benefit of colonial powers, with little regard for the development of local economies or the well-being of indigenous populations. This pattern of resource extraction without equitable distribution has persisted in many African nations even after independence.

2. Governance Challenges And Corruption

Weak governance structures, political instability, and widespread corruption have plagued many African nations, leading to the mismanagement of resources and the concentration of wealth in the hands of a few elites. Corruption has diverted resources from critical sectors such as education, healthcare, and infrastructure development, further exacerbating poverty and underdevelopment.

3. Resource Curse and Dutch Disease

The abundance of natural resources, particularly in the extractive industries, has paradoxically contributed to economic stagnation and underdevelopment in some African nations. The "resource curse" phenomenon, where resource wealth leads to a reliance on exports, currency appreciation, and the neglect of other economic sectors, has hindered diversification and sustainable economic growth.

4. Conflict And Instability

Conflicts over resource control, ethnic tensions, and political instability have plagued several African nations, disrupting economic activities, displacing populations, and diverting resources away from development efforts. The negative impacts of conflicts on infrastructure, human capital, and investor confidence have perpetuated cycles of poverty and underdevelopment.

5. Unfavorable Trade Agreements and External Factors

Africa's integration into the global economy has often been on unfavorable terms, with trade agreements and policies favoring more developed nations. Additionally, external factors such as fluctuations in commodity prices, climate change, and global economic downturns have significantly impacted African economies, exacerbating poverty and inequality.

We Can Overcome

Overcoming the paradox of wealth and poverty in Africa requires a multifaceted approach that addresses these underlying challenges. This may involve:

1. Strengthening governance and accountability mechanisms to combat corruption and ensure the equitable distribution of resource wealth.

2. Diversifying economies and promoting value-addition industries to reduce reliance on raw material exports and mitigate the resource curse.

3. Investing in human capital development through improved access to education, healthcare, and skills training.

4. Promoting regional integration and intra-African trade to create larger markets and foster economic growth.

5. Adopting sustainable resource management practices and investing in renewable energy sources to mitigate environmental degradation and climate change impacts.

6. Fostering political stability, conflict resolution, and peacebuilding efforts to create an enabling environment for economic development.

7. Engaging in fair and balanced trade agreements and partnerships that promote African interests and sustainable development.

Addressing the paradox of wealth and poverty in Africa requires a concerted effort from African governments, regional organizations, international partners, and the global community. By leveraging the continent's abundant resources responsibly and equitably, while addressing the underlying structural challenges, Africa can unlock its immense potential and achieve sustainable and inclusive development for its people.

The Promise of Prosperity

Africa's natural endowments are the envy of the world, holding the potential to catapult the continent into a new era of prosperity. With vast reserves of oil, gas, minerals, and arable land, Africa possesses the building blocks for sustainable development and economic growth. From the agricultural heartlands of the Nile Delta to the mineral-rich veins of the Congo Basin, the continent's wealth is as boundless as its horizons.

Strategic Steps for Africa to Harness Its Rich Resources

Africa, a continent blessed with an abundance of natural resources and human potential, has long grappled with the paradox of wealth and poverty. However, the path to prosperity lies in harnessing these resources strategically and overcoming the challenges that have hindered its development. By learning from the experiences of other nations that have successfully transformed their economies, Africa can unlock its promise of prosperity. The following should help Africa become great in commensuration to its abundant resources.

1. Fostering Good Governance and Institutional Reforms:

Transparent and accountable governance is critical for the effective management of natural resources and the equitable distribution of wealth. Africa must prioritize strengthening democratic institutions, combating corruption, and promoting the rule of law. The examples of Botswana and Singapore, which have leveraged their resource wealth through strong governance and anti-corruption measures, serve as models for Africa.

2. Diversifying Economies and Promoting Value-Addition:

Over-reliance on raw material exports has often been a curse for resource-rich nations. Africa must diversify its economies by developing value-added industries, such as manufacturing, agro-processing, and technology sectors. Countries like Malaysia and South Korea successfully transitioned from commodity-based economies to industrialized nations through strategic economic diversification and investment in human capital.

3. Investing in Human Capital and Infrastructure:

Sustainable development requires a skilled and healthy workforce, as well as robust infrastructure to support economic activities. Africa should prioritize investments in education, healthcare, and infrastructure development, following the examples of nations like Singapore and South Korea, which have reaped the benefits of investing in their human resources and physical infrastructure.

4. Promoting Regional Integration and Intra-African Trade:

Africa's fragmented markets and barriers to intra-regional trade have hindered economic growth. By fostering regional integration, harmonizing policies, and reducing trade barriers, African nations can create larger markets for goods and services, as exemplified by the success of regional blocs like the European Union and the Association of Southeast Asian Nations (ASEAN).

5. Embracing Sustainable Resource Management:

Africa's natural resources are finite, and their exploitation must be balanced with environmental sustainability. Adopting sustainable resource management practices, investing in renewable energy sources, and promoting a green economy can safeguard Africa's ecological wealth while creating new economic opportunities. Countries like Costa Rica and Norway have demonstrated how sustainable resource management can contribute to long-term prosperity.

6. Leveraging Public-Private Partnerships and Foreign Direct Investment:

Mobilizing domestic resources alone may not be sufficient for Africa's development needs. By creating an enabling environment for private sector participation and attracting responsible foreign direct investment, Africa can tap into much-needed capital, technology, and expertise. Countries like China and India have leveraged public-private partnerships and foreign investment to drive economic growth.

7. Fostering Innovation and Entrepreneurship:

Africa's youth represent a reservoir of talent and creativity that must be nurtured. By promoting innovation ecosystems, supporting entrepreneurship, and leveraging emerging technologies, Africa can unlock new economic opportunities and create sustainable jobs. Israel and South Korea exemplify how fostering innovation and entrepreneurship can drive economic transformation.

The path to prosperity is not without challenges, but Africa can draw inspiration from the success stories of nations that have overcome similar obstacles. By implementing these strategic steps, Africa can harness its rich resources, unlock its potential, and usher in an era of inclusive and sustainable development for its people.

We can refer to the Niger Delta in Nigeria, home to one of the world's largest oil reserves, and its potential to fuel economic development and alleviate poverty.

The Plague of Resource Curse

Yet, for all its riches, Africa finds itself ensnared in the clutches of the resource curse, a phenomenon that sees mineral wealth become a curse rather than a blessing. From the diamond fields of Sierra Leone to the gold mines of Ghana, resource-rich nations are plagued by corruption, conflict, and environmental degradation. The scramble for control over lucrative resources fuels violent conflicts, undermines democratic institutions, and lines the pockets of corrupt elites while leaving the masses in poverty.

Why Abundant Resources Have Become a Problem in Africa

The phenomenon known as the "resource curse" has plagued many resource-rich nations, particularly in Africa, where the abundance of natural resources has paradoxically become a hindrance to economic development and prosperity. Instead of serving as a blessing, the wealth of resources has often fueled corruption, conflict, and economic stagnation. Here are some reasons why the resource curse has taken hold in many parts of Africa:

1. Overdependence on Resource Exports:

Many African economies have become overly reliant on the export of raw materials such as oil, minerals, and agricultural commodities. This dependence has hindered diversification and made these economies highly vulnerable to commodity price fluctuations and external shocks.

2. Dutch Disease:

The influx of resource wealth can lead to an appreciation of the local currency, making other sectors of the economy, such as manufacturing and agriculture, less competitive. This "Dutch disease" effect can undermine economic diversification and contribute to deindustrialization.

3. Corruption and Mismanagement:

The high economic stakes associated with natural resource extraction have created fertile ground for corruption and mismanagement. Revenues from resource exports have often been siphoned off by ruling elites or misallocated, instead of being reinvested in productive sectors and infrastructure for sustainable development.

4. Weak Governance and Institutional Frameworks:

Many resource-rich African nations lack strong institutions, accountability mechanisms, and transparent regulatory frameworks to manage their resource wealth effectively. This has enabled rent-seeking behavior, cronyism, and the concentration of power and wealth in the hands of a few.

5. Resource-Related Conflicts:

The competition for control over valuable natural resources has fueled conflicts, civil wars, and instability in several African nations. These conflicts have not only caused immense human suffering but have also disrupted economic activities, deterred investment, and diverted resources away from development priorities.

6. Environmental Degradation:

The extraction of natural resources, especially in the mining and oil sectors, has often been accompanied by environmental degradation, pollution, and the displacement of local communities. This has undermined sustainable development and posed long-term risks to the well-being of affected populations.

7. Neglect of Human Capital Development:

The resource curse has also led to the neglect of investments in education, healthcare, and other forms of human capital development. This has hindered the development of a skilled workforce and limited the potential for economic diversification and innovation.

To break the curse of resource abundance, African nations must address these underlying challenges through a combination of institutional reforms, good governance, diversification strategies, and sustainable resource management practices. Lessons can be drawn from countries like Norway and Botswana, which have managed their resource wealth more effectively by establishing sovereign wealth funds, promoting transparency, and investing in human capital and economic diversification.

Ultimately, the path to prosperity lies in transforming Africa's natural resource wealth into a catalyst for inclusive and sustainable development, rather than allowing it to become a curse that perpetuates poverty, inequality, and economic stagnation.

Reference to the civil wars in Sierra Leone and Liberia, fueled by the illicit trade in conflict diamonds, and their devastating impact on civilian populations.

Customary Corruption

At the heart of Africa's economic woes lies the insidious specter of corruption, a cancer that eats away at the fabric of society and erodes trust in public institutions. From petty bribery to grand embezzlement, corruption permeates every level of governance, diverting precious resources away from essential services and into the pockets of the privileged few. The endemic nature of corruption stifles entrepreneurship, discourages foreign investment, and perpetuates cycles of poverty and inequality.

The Cancer of Society

Corruption, a malignant force that erodes the foundations of society, has emerged as a formidable obstacle to Africa's path to prosperity. Like a cancer that metastasizes and spreads, corruption has infiltrated various sectors, crippling economies and undermining the potential of entire nations. The misuse of power for personal gain has become a scourge that impedes development, perpetuates poverty, and undermines the rule of law.

The annals of African history are replete with examples of leaders who, through corruption, have squandered their nations' resources and stifled economic growth. One such example is Mobutu Sese Seko, the former president of Zaire (now the Democratic Republic of Congo). During his three-decade reign, Mobutu systematically looted the country's wealth, embezzling billions of dollars and amassing a personal fortune estimated at $5 billion. His kleptocratic regime drained the nation's coffers, leaving its infrastructure in shambles and its people mired in abject poverty.

Another notorious case is that of Sani Abacha, the former military dictator of Nigeria. During his five-year rule, Abacha and his associates are believed to have embezzled between $3 billion and $5 billion from the country's oil revenues. This massive corruption scandal not only deprived Nigeria of crucial resources for development but also tarnished the country's international reputation, hindering foreign investment and economic progress.

In Zimbabwe, the reign of Robert Mugabe, the country's former president, was marred by widespread corruption and economic mismanagement. Mugabe's policies, including the controversial land reform program, led to the collapse of the agricultural sector and severe economic decline. Additionally, his inner circle was accused of siphoning off state funds and resources for personal enrichment, exacerbating the country's economic woes.

The consequences of corruption extend far beyond economic losses. It undermines the trust of citizens in their government, erodes the rule of law, and perpetuates a culture of impunity. Corruption also deters foreign investment, as investors are reluctant to engage in economies plagued by graft and lack of transparency.

Fighting the Monster

Combating corruption requires a multifaceted approach involving strong institutions, effective accountability mechanisms, and a commitment to the rule of law. Transparency International, a global coalition against corruption, has advocated for measures such as the establishment of independent anti-corruption agencies, the protection of whistleblowers, and the implementation of robust asset recovery frameworks.

Moreover, the involvement of civil society, the media, and the private sector is crucial in fostering a culture of accountability and integrity. Education and public awareness campaigns can also play a vital role in empowering citizens to demand transparency and hold their leaders accountable.

Eradicating corruption is a daunting task, but it is a battle that Africans must win for Africa to realize its full potential. By stemming the tide of corruption, nations can unlock resources for sustainable development, attract foreign investment, and foster an environment conducive to economic growth and social progress.

Transparency International's Corruption Perceptions Index consistently ranks many African nations among the most corrupt in the world.

Institutionalized Inequality

As wealth flows into the coffers of the elite, the gap between rich and poor widens, creating chasms of inequality that divide societies and undermine social cohesion. From the gated enclaves of the super-rich to the sprawling slums that stretch as far as the eye can see, Africa's cities are microcosms of this stark divide. The concentration of wealth and power in the hands of a privileged few leaves the majority of Africans marginalized and excluded from the fruits of economic progress.

The Great Divide

The stark disparities that exist within and among nations have given rise to a great divide, one that threatens the very fabric of societies and undermines the principles of justice and human dignity. This inequality, a persistent and pervasive force, manifests itself in various forms, from economic deprivation to social marginalization and political disenfranchisement.

In Africa, the scourge of inequality has been a lingering legacy of colonialism, exacerbated by factors such as corruption, conflict, and inadequate access to education and healthcare. The wealth gap between the privileged few and the impoverished masses has widened, creating a chasm that perpetuates cycles of poverty, disempowerment, and social unrest.

Addressing this great divide requires a multifaceted approach that acknowledges the inherent dignity and worth of every human being, regardless of his or her circumstances. At the heart of this endeavor lies the pursuit of equality before the law, a fundamental principle that establishes a level playing field and ensures that all individuals are treated with fairness and impartiality.

Resolving the Inequalities

To resolve inequality and make all men equal in the eyes of the law, practical steps must be taken:

1. Strengthening the Rule of Law:

Robust legal frameworks and independent judiciaries are essential for upholding the principles of equality and non-discrimination. By ensuring that laws are applied equitably and without bias, societies can foster an environment of trust and accountability.

2. Promoting Inclusive Economic Policies:

Economic policies that prioritize inclusive growth, sustainable development, and equitable distribution of resources are crucial for reducing disparities. This may involve initiatives such as progressive taxation, access to affordable healthcare and education, and support for small and medium-sized enterprises.

3. Empowering Marginalized Groups:

Targeted efforts must be made to empower groups that have historically faced discrimination and exclusion, such as women, ethnic minorities, and persons with disabilities. This can include programs that promote equal opportunities in education, employment, and political participation.

4. Investing in Human Capital:

Education is a powerful tool for breaking cycles of poverty and inequality. By investing in quality education and vocational training programs, nations can equip their citizens with the skills and knowledge necessary to participate fully in the economic and social spheres.

5. Fostering Inclusive Governance:

Inclusive and participatory governance structures are essential for ensuring that all voices are heard and that decision-making processes reflect the diverse needs and aspirations of the populace. This may involve measures such as decentralization, public consultations, and the promotion of civic engagement.

6. Addressing Systemic Barriers:

It is imperative to identify and dismantle systemic barriers that perpetuate inequality, such as discrimination in hiring practices, gender-based violence, and limited access to financial services. Comprehensive policies and awareness campaigns can help tackle these deep-rooted challenges.

The pursuit of equality before the law is a noble and necessary endeavor, one that demands unwavering commitment and collective action. By embracing these practical steps, nations can bridge the great divide, foster social cohesion, and unlock the full potential of their citizens, creating a more just and prosperous society for all.

The Gini coefficient, which measures income inequality, revealing stark disparities within African nations and across the continent, as a whole is a strong reference.

Navigating the Nexus of Wealth and Want in Africa

Africa, a continent endowed with an abundance of natural resources and immense potential, has long grappled with the paradoxical coexistence of wealth and want. This stark contrast, where pockets of affluence exist alongside widespread poverty and deprivation, has become a defining feature of many African nations.

At the heart of this dichotomy lies a complex web of historical, political, economic, and social factors that have shaped the continent's development trajectory. The legacy of colonialism, coupled with poor governance, corruption, and conflicts, has hindered the equitable distribution of wealth and the effective utilization of resources for the betterment of all citizens.

Navigating this nexus of wealth and want requires a multifaceted approach that addresses the root causes of inequality and fosters inclusive and sustainable development. Here are some key considerations:

1. Resource Governance and Transparency

Africa's abundant natural resources have often been a source of both wealth and conflict. Establishing robust governance frameworks, promoting transparency, and combating corruption in the extractive industries are crucial steps towards ensuring that resource revenues benefit the broader population.

2. Economic diversification

Over-reliance on raw material exports has left many African economies vulnerable to commodity price fluctuations and the "resource curse." Diversifying economies through industrialization, value-addition, and the development of service sectors can create sustainable and inclusive growth opportunities.

3. Human capital development

Investing in quality education, healthcare, and skills training is essential for empowering individuals and communities to participate actively in economic activities and break intergenerational cycles of poverty.

4. Infrastructure and connectivity

Bridging the infrastructure gap by developing reliable transportation networks, energy systems, and digital connectivity can unlock economic potential, facilitate trade, and improve access to essential services.

5. Inclusive governance and policy-making

Ensuring that marginalized groups, including women, youth, and rural communities, have a voice in decision-making processes and access to opportunities is crucial for fostering inclusive development and social cohesion.

6. Regional integration and cooperation

By promoting intra-African trade, harmonizing policies, and fostering regional cooperation, African nations can create larger markets, leverage economies of scale, and address cross-border challenges more effectively.

7. Sustainable resource management

Balancing economic growth with environmental sustainability is paramount for preserving Africa's natural wealth for future generations. Embracing sustainable practices, investing in renewable energy, and promoting climate resilience can mitigate the adverse impacts of environmental degradation.

Navigating the nexus of wealth and want in Africa is a complex and multifaceted challenge, but one that must be addressed with urgency and determination. By leveraging the continent's immense resources responsibly and equitably, while addressing the underlying structural inequalities, African nations can forge a path towards inclusive prosperity, where the benefits of development are shared by all.

As Africa grapples with the paradox of plenty amidst poverty, the path forward is fraught with challenges and opportunities. To unlock the continent's potential and fulfill the aspirations of its people, we must confront the root causes of economic injustice with determination and resolve. Only by addressing the scourge of corruption, bridging the gap between rich and poor, and harnessing the continent's wealth for the benefit of all can we hope to build a future where Africa's riches are shared equitably and its promise fulfilled.

CHAPTER 3

THE TYRANNY OF BAD LEADERSHIP

SHADOWS OF TYRANNY

In the labyrinthine corridors of power across Africa, the specter of bad leadership casts a long shadow over the hopes and aspirations of millions. From the opulent palaces of autocrats to the crumbling institutions of fragile democracies, the legacy of despotic rule looms large, stifling progress and strangling the promise of a better tomorrow.

The Anatomy of Autocracy

Autocracy, a system of government characterized by concentrated power and authority in the hands of a single ruler or a small elite group, has plagued numerous nations across the globe, stifling progress and perpetuating injustice. The origins of autocratic regimes can often be traced back to a complex interplay of historical, political, and socio-economic factors that have facilitated the consolidation of power and the suppression of dissent.

In Africa, the legacy of colonialism played a pivotal role in shaping the trajectory of many nations toward autocratic rule. Colonial powers, driven by their own interests, often installed or supported leaders who would safeguard their economic and strategic interests, disregarding the aspirations of the local populace. This practice sowed the seeds of authoritarianism, as these leaders sought to maintain their grip on power by any means necessary.

Moreover, the arbitrary borders drawn by colonial powers, often disregarding ethnic and cultural boundaries, created fertile ground for ethnic tensions and conflicts, which autocratic leaders exploited to solidify their rule. By portraying themselves as the sole guarantors of stability and unity, these leaders justified their iron-fisted tactics and suppressed dissent under the guise of preserving national security.

The demerits of autocratic rule are numerous and far-reaching, undermining the very foundations of democratic governance and human rights. Firstly, autocracies are inherently antithetical to the principles of accountability and transparency, as power is concentrated in the hands of a few, with limited checks and balances. This environment fosters corruption, nepotism, and the misappropriation of public resources for personal gain.

Secondly, autocratic regimes often rely on repression and the curtailment of civil liberties to maintain their grip on power. Freedom of speech, freedom of assembly, and freedom of the press are routinely violated, stifling dissent and silencing critical voices. This climate of fear and intimidation erodes the fabric of society, fostering mistrust and resentment among the populace.

Thirdly, economic stagnation and inefficiency are the factors that typically characterize autocracies. Without genuine competition, innovation, and meritocracy, resources are often misallocated, and economic opportunities are limited to a privileged few with ties to the ruling elite. This perpetuates inequality, poverty, and social unrest, further entrenching the autocratic system.

Furthermore, autocratic regimes are inherently unstable, as they lack the mechanisms for peaceful transitions of power and are often plagued by internal power struggles and succession crises. This instability can lead to civil unrest, violence, and even armed conflicts, as competing factions vie for control.

Breaking Free

To break free from the shackles of autocracy, African nations must embrace the principles of democracy, good governance, and respect for human rights. This requires the strengthening of democratic institutions, the promotion of free and fair elections, and the empowerment of civil society organizations and independent media.

Additionally, addressing the root causes of autocracy, such as ethnic tensions, economic inequality, and lack of educational opportunities, is crucial for fostering a stable and inclusive political landscape. Furthermore, by promoting national reconciliation, investing in human capital, and fostering economic development, nations can create an environment where people no longer see autocracy as unavoidable but rather an anachronistic and oppressive system that impedes progress.

The path towards dismantling autocracy may be arduous, but a journey that we must undertake for the sake of human dignity, justice, and the realization of the continent's vast potential.

At the heart of Africa's governance woes lies the scourge of autocracy, where leaders wield absolute power with impunity, crushing dissent and quashing opposition in their relentless pursuit of self-aggrandizement. From the megalomaniacal excesses of dictators like Mobutu Sese Seko and Idi Amin to the subtle authoritarianism of elected demagogues, the continent has borne witness to a litany of despots who rule with an iron fist, plundering national coffers and trampling on human rights.

The reign of Robert Mugabe in Zimbabwe, characterized by decades of repression, economic mismanagement, and electoral fraud, emblematic of autocratic rule in Africa.

The Mirage of Democracy in Africa

Across the African continent, the promise of democracy has often been elusive, a mirage that tantalizingly appears on the horizon, only to dissolve into an illusion of genuine political freedom and representation. Despite the adoption of democratic structures and the holding of periodic elections, many nations in Africa continue to grapple with the challenges of entrenched authoritarian tendencies, electoral irregularities, and the concentration of power in the hands of a few.

The reasons behind this mirage of democracy are multifaceted and deeply rooted in the continent's complex historical, political, and socio-economic landscape. Here are some key factors contributing to the fragility of democratic institutions in Africa:

1. Colonial legacy and neo-patrimonialism

The legacy of colonialism has left a lasting imprint on many African nations, shaping their political systems and power dynamics. The practice of neo-patrimonialism, where political authority is based on the exchange of personal favors and the distribution of state resources to maintain loyalty, has persisted, undermining the principles of accountability and meritocracy.

2. Ethnic tensions and conflicts

The arbitrary borders drawn by colonial powers often divided ethnic groups or forced diverse communities to coexist within the same national boundaries. Political elites, fueling divisive rhetoric and undermining the development of cohesive national identities and inclusive democratic processes, have exploited these ethnic tensions and conflicts.

3. Weak institutions and rule of law

Many African nations lack robust democratic institutions, independent judiciaries, and effective checks and balances on executive power. This institutional weakness has enabled the concentration of power, abuse of authority, and the erosion of the rule of law, rendering democratic processes vulnerable to manipulation and subversion.

4. Economic challenges and resource curse

Poverty, inequality, and the over-reliance on natural resource extraction have created environments where political power is perceived as a means to access wealth and resources. This has fueled corruption, rent-seeking behavior, and the entrenchment of authoritarian regimes that prioritize personal enrichment over democratic principles.

5. External interference and geopolitical interests

External actors, including former colonial powers and global superpowers, have at times supported or enabled authoritarian regimes in Africa, prioritizing their own strategic interests over the promotion of genuine democracy and human rights.

6. Leadership deficit and lack of democratic culture

The absence of a strong democratic culture and the dearth of principled, visionary leadership committed to the ideals of democracy have hampered the consolidation of democratic institutions and practices in many African nations.

Overcoming the mirage of democracy in Africa requires a multifaceted approach that addresses these deep-rooted challenges. This may involve strengthening democratic institutions, promoting inclusive governance, fostering economic development and diversification, resolving ethnic tensions through dialogue and reconciliation, and cultivating a democratic political culture through civic education and empowerment.

Additionally, regional and international organizations can play a crucial role in supporting democratic processes, monitoring elections, and holding leaders accountable to their commitments to democratic principles and human rights.

Ultimately, the realization of genuine democracy in Africa hinges on the collective efforts of governments, civil society, and the international community, as well as a shared commitment to the values of freedom, equality, and justice for all.

The disputed elections in Kenya in 2007, marred by allegations of fraud and violence, and the subsequent political crisis that engulfed the nation, highlighting the fragility of democratic institutions.

Nepotism and Patronage in Africa

The scourges of nepotism and patronage have long plagued the political and economic landscapes of many African nations, undermining meritocracy, fostering corruption, and hindering equitable development. These intertwined practices, rooted in complex historical and cultural factors, have become deeply entrenched, perpetuating a cycle of cronyism and the concentration of power and resources in the hands of a privileged few.

Nepotism, the practice of favoring relatives or close associates for positions of power or employment, has been a persistent challenge across the continent. In many African societies, kinship ties and extended family networks hold significant cultural significance, often taking precedence over formal qualifications or merit-based selection processes. This has led to the appointment of unqualified individuals to critical positions, compromising the efficiency and effectiveness of public institutions and private enterprises.

Closely linked to nepotism is the phenomenon of patronage, a system of reciprocal exchange in which political leaders distribute state resources, contracts, and positions of influence to secure loyalty and maintain their power base. This practice has been exacerbated by the neo-patrimonial tendencies that persist in many African states, where the lines between public and private spheres are often blurred, and state resources are treated as personal possessions.

The reasons behind the prevalence of nepotism and patronage in Africa are multifaceted and deeply rooted in the continent's historical and socio-cultural fabric:

1. Colonial Legacy

The legacy of colonial rule and the imposition of arbitrary borders often disrupted traditional governance systems, leading to the concentration of power and the emergence of patronage networks as a means of maintaining control and securing allegiances.

2. Ethnic and Tribal Loyalties

In the absence of strong national identities, ethnic and tribal loyalties have played a significant role in shaping political alliances and patronage networks, as leaders seek to consolidate their support base along ethnic lines.

3. Poverty and Economic Insecurity

High levels of poverty and economic insecurity have fueled the desire for access to state resources and employment opportunities, leading individuals to seek the patronage of those in power as a means of survival and advancement.

4. Weak Institutions and Lack of Accountability

The absence of robust and rich democratic institutions, effective checks and balances, and accountability mechanisms has enabled the perpetuation of nepotism and patronage, with little consequence for those engaging in such practices.

5. Cultural and Social Norms

In some African societies, the concepts of reciprocity and loyalty to extended family networks are deeply ingrained, leading to the acceptance and normalization of nepotistic practices.

The consequences of nepotism and patronage are far-reaching and detrimental to the development of African nations. These practices undermine meritocracy, leading to the appointment of unqualified individuals to positions of importance, compromising service delivery and economic productivity. They also fuel corruption, as resources are diverted for personal gain and the interests of the patronage network, rather than being utilized for the greater public good.

Addressing these challenges requires a multifaceted approach that involves strengthening democratic institutions, promoting transparency and accountability, fostering economic development and social mobility, and cultivating a cultural shift towards meritocracy and ethical governance. Additionally, efforts to promote national unity and inclusive identities can help mitigate the influence of ethnic and tribal loyalties in perpetuating patronage networks.

While the path towards eradicating nepotism and patronage in Africa is arduous, it is a necessary journey for the continent to realize its full potential and achieve equitable and sustainable development for all its citizens.

The reign of Muammar Gaddafi in Libya, where his family members held key positions of power and benefited from the country's vast oil wealth at the expense of the Libyan people remains a valid example.

The Price of Dissent

For those brave enough to speak out against the tyranny of bad leadership, the price of dissent can be steep, as journalists, activists, and political opponents are silenced through intimidation, harassment, and violence. From the crackdown on independent media outlets to the arbitrary detention of human rights defenders, the space for civil society to operate freely is shrinking, leaving few avenues for peaceful resistance in the face of tyranny.

Opposition to Bad Tyranny in African Nations: Pain versus Prospect

Across the African continent, the path of opposition to authoritarian rule and tyranny has often been fraught with immense personal sacrifices, persecution, and even loss of life. Those who dare to challenge the status quo and stand up against oppressive regimes have faced dire consequences, underscoring the lengths to which some leaders will go to maintain their grip on power.

One of the most poignant examples is that of Patrice Lumumba, the first democratically elected Prime Minister of the Democratic Republic of Congo (then known as the Belgian Congo). Lumumba's vocal opposition to Belgian colonial rule and his efforts to assert the nation's independence and sovereignty were perceived as a threat by both Belgian authorities and Western powers. In 1961, he was arrested, brutally beaten, and ultimately executed. His body dismembered and dissolved in acid, a chilling testament to the brutality inflicted upon those who dared to defy entrenched interests.

In South Africa, the struggle against the oppressive apartheid regime claimed countless lives, with leaders like Steve Biko and countless others paying the ultimate price for their activism. Biko, a prominent figure in the Black Consciousness Movement, was arrested and subjected to torture by the South African security forces in 1977. He sustained massive head injuries during his detention and died shortly thereafter, becoming a martyr in the fight against racial segregation and injustice.

The city of Addis Ababa, Ethiopia, has witnessed its share of opposition to tyranny, with the notorious "Red Terror" campaign waged by the Derg military junta in the late 1970s. Thousands of innocent civilians, including students, intellectuals, and political dissidents, were brutally murdered for their perceived opposition to the regime, their bodies often left displayed in public as a grim warning to others.

In Zimbabwe, the late Morgan Tsvangirai, a prominent opposition leader and former Prime Minister, faced numerous arrests, beatings, and attempts on his life for his defiance of Robert

Mugabe's authoritarian rule. In 2007, he was brutally assaulted by police during a peaceful protest, sustaining serious injuries that required medical treatment abroad.

The examples are numerous and span the continent, from the assassination of Thomas Sankara, the revolutionary leader of Burkina Faso, to the imprisonment and harassment of opposition figures like Leah Sharibu in Nigeria and Bobi Wine in Uganda.

The price of opposition to bad tyranny in African nations has been steep, with countless individuals sacrificing their freedom, their well-being, and even their lives in the pursuit of justice, democracy, and human rights. Their stories serve as a sobering reminder of the resilience and courage required to challenge entrenched power structures and the depths to which some leaders will sink to maintain their grip on power.

Charting a Path to Liberation in Africa

The struggle for liberation from oppressive and authoritarian regimes in Africa has been long and arduous, with many brave individuals sacrificing their lives in pursuit of freedom, justice, and human rights. While the path to overthrowing the cabals in government may seem daunting, there are legitimate and non-violent ways to chart a course towards true liberation.

1. Grassroots Mobilization and Civil Resistance

One of the most powerful tools in the struggle for liberation is the mobilization of the masses through peaceful civil resistance. By harnessing the power of collective action, ordinary citizens can challenge the status quo and demand change through non-violent means such as protests, strikes, and civil disobedience campaigns. Examples like the anti-apartheid movement in South Africa and the Sudanese revolution of 2019 demonstrate the potency of sustained, non-violent resistance in undermining the grip of authoritarian regimes.

2. Building Strong Democratic Institutions

The consolidation of democratic institutions is crucial for ensuring long-term stability and preventing the resurgence of authoritarianism. This involves strengthening the rule of law, promoting transparency and accountability, and fostering an independent judiciary and media. By empowering civil society organizations, promoting civic education, and upholding the principles of checks and balances, African nations can lay the foundation for a more just and equitable political system.

3. Economic Empowerment and Inclusive Development

Addressing the root causes of social and economic inequality is vital in dismantling the power structures that sustain oppressive regimes. By promoting inclusive economic policies, fostering entrepreneurship, and investing in education and healthcare, African nations can create opportunities for upward mobility and empower marginalized communities to participate fully in the political process. This can help undermine the patronage networks and cronyism that often prop up authoritarian rulers.

4. Regional and International Cooperation

The struggle for liberation in Africa cannot be waged in isolation. Regional and international cooperation is essential in exerting pressure on oppressive regimes and supporting democratic movements. Organizations like the African Union (AU) and the United Nations (UN) can play a vital role in monitoring human rights violations, imposing targeted sanctions, and facilitating dialogue and conflict resolution. Additionally, the solidarity and support of the global community can amplify the voices of those fighting for freedom and democracy.

5. Principled and Ethical Leadership

Ultimately, the success of any liberation movement hinges on the emergence of principled and ethical leaders who are committed to the values of democracy, human rights, and the rule of law. These leaders must not only inspire and mobilize the masses but also embody the ideals they espouse, rejecting corruption, nepotism, and the abuse of power. By cultivating a new generation of visionary and selfless leaders, African nations can break the cycle of authoritarianism and pave the way for a more just and prosperous future.

It is important to note that while the path to liberation may involve civil resistance and political activism, any resort to violence or unconstitutional means undermines the very principles of democracy and human rights that the struggle seeks to uphold. The road to freedom is long and arduous, but it is through perseverance, unity, and a commitment to non-violent resistance that the cabals of oppression can be dismantled and a new era of liberation ushered in.

CHAPTER 4

Economic Mismanagement and Its Consequences

A CYCLE OF SQUANDERED OPPORTUNITIES

Africa, a continent endowed with immense natural resources, cultural richness, and a vibrant youth population, has been trapped in a vicious cycle of squandered opportunities, hindering its ability to realize its full potential and achieve sustainable development. This cycle, perpetuated by a multitude of factors, has resulted in stagnation, poverty, and the perpetuation of inequalities across many nations on the continent.

One of the most glaring manifestations of this cycle is the mismanagement and exploitation of Africa's vast natural resources. Despite the abundance of minerals, oil, gas, and fertile lands, the benefits of these resources have often been concentrated in the hands of a privileged few, while the majority of the population remains impoverished. Corruption, weak governance structures, and the resource curse phenomenon have led to the squandering of these opportunities for inclusive economic growth and development.

Furthermore, the legacy of colonialism and its aftermath have contributed significantly to the cycle of squandered opportunities. The arbitrary borders drawn during the colonial era have fueled ethnic tensions and conflicts, diverting precious resources towards violence and instability instead of nation-building and development. The extraction of wealth and the suppression of indigenous knowledge systems during colonial rule have also left a lasting impact, hampering the ability of African nations to chart their own path to progress.

Political instability, authoritarianism, and the lack of democratic institutions have also played a significant role in perpetuating this cycle. Countries mired in conflicts, human rights abuses, and the concentration of power in the hands of a few elites have struggled to create an enabling environment for economic growth, social progress, and the empowerment of their citizens.

The squandering of opportunities extends to the realm of human capital development as well. Inadequate investments in education, healthcare, and skills training have hindered the ability of African nations to nurture and unleash the potential of their youth. This, in turn, has perpetuated intergenerational cycles of poverty, limited access to opportunities and brain drain as talented individuals seek greener pastures elsewhere.

Moreover, the lack of regional integration, infrastructure deficits, and barriers to intra-African trade have further exacerbated the cycle of squandered opportunities. The fragmentation of markets, the high costs of trade, and the inability to leverage economies of scale have hindered the continent's ability to harness its collective potential and compete effectively in the global economy.

Breaking this cycle of squandered opportunities requires a multi-pronged approach that addresses the root causes of the challenges facing Africa. This includes strengthening governance and democratic institutions, promoting transparency and accountability, investing in human capital development, fostering regional integration and intra-African trade, and embracing sustainable resource management practices.

Additionally, it is crucial to address the legacies of colonialism, promote reconciliation and national unity, and empower marginalized communities to participate fully in the development process. By recognizing and addressing these long-standing issues, African nations can begin to transform the cycle of squandered opportunities into a cycle of progress, prosperity, and self-determination.

The path ahead is not without challenges, but by harnessing the resilience, creativity, and determination of its people, Africa can break free from the shackles of the past and chart a new course towards a brighter future, where they can seize opportunities and realize their potentials for the benefit of all.

The Legacy of Dependency

Africa's economic woes are rooted in a history of dependency, where colonial exploitation gave rise to a pattern of economic subjugation that persists to this day. From cash crop monocultures to extractive industries dominated by foreign corporations, the continent's economies remain shackled to a legacy of exploitation that enriches outsiders while leaving Africans trapped in a cycle of poverty.

The exploitation of African labor and resources by European colonial powers, laid the foundation for a global economic order that continues to disadvantage African nations. (add...)

The Legacy of Dependency and Paths to Self-Reliance for African Nations

The legacy of dependency on the Western world has been a persistent challenge for many African nations, hampering their ability to chart their own course and achieve true self-determination. This dependency, rooted in the historical legacy of colonialism and the unequal power dynamics that emerged in its aftermath, has manifested in various forms, including economic, political, and cultural spheres.

Economically, many African nations have remained heavily reliant on the export of raw materials and primary commodities to Western markets, perpetuating a cycle of dependency and vulnerability to global market fluctuations. This extractive economic model has often led to the neglect of domestic industries, limited value addition, and a perpetuation of poverty and underdevelopment.

Politically, the influence of Western powers and their geopolitical interests have often shaped the trajectories of African nations, sometimes supporting authoritarian regimes or imposing conditions that undermine national sovereignty. This external interference has hindered the development of truly independent and representative governance structures that prioritize the needs and aspirations of the African people.

Culturally, the legacy of colonialism has led to the marginalization and erosion of indigenous knowledge systems, values, and traditions, contributing to a sense of disconnection and dependency on Western ideologies and belief systems.

Breaking free from this legacy of dependency and fostering self-reliance requires a multifaceted approach that addresses the root causes of this phenomenon and empowers African nations to chart their own path to sustainable development.

1. Economic Diversification and Industrialization

African nations must prioritize economic diversification and industrialization, moving away from an over-reliance on raw material exports. By developing value-added industries, promoting local manufacturing, and fostering entrepreneurship, nations can reduce their vulnerability to external shocks and create sustainable economic opportunities for their citizens.

2. Regional Integration and Intra-African Trade

Strengthening regional integration and boosting intra-African trade can create larger markets, leverage economies of scale, and reduce dependency on external markets. By harmonizing policies, removing trade barriers, and investing in regional infrastructure, African nations can foster mutually beneficial economic cooperation and self-reliance.

3. Investing in Human Capital and Indigenous Knowledge Systems

Prioritizing investments in education, skills training, and healthcare is crucial for nurturing a skilled and productive workforce that can drive innovation and development. Additionally, recognizing and revitalizing indigenous knowledge systems, promoting cultural preservation, and fostering a sense of pride in African heritage can contribute to a more self-reliant and resilient society.

4. Strengthening Democratic Institutions and Good Governance

Consolidating democratic institutions, promoting transparency and accountability, and upholding the rule of law are essential for ensuring that leaders who prioritize the interests of their citizens govern African nations. Strong governance frameworks can also help to reduce external interference and foster greater self-determination.

5. Fostering Strategic Partnerships and South-South Cooperation

While reducing dependency on the West, African nations can explore strategic partnerships and cooperation with other developing nations, particularly in the Global South. Such partnerships can facilitate the exchange of knowledge, resources, and best practices, fostering mutual growth and self-reliance.

6. Promoting Sustainable Resource Management

Adopting sustainable practices in the management of natural resources can help to ensure that Africa's wealth is harnessed for the benefit of current and future generations, reducing dependency on external actors and promoting long-term self-reliance.

Breaking the legacy of dependency is a complex and multifaceted challenge, but one that is essential for African nations to truly realize their potential and achieve sustainable development. By embracing these strategies and fostering a mindset of self-reliance, African nations can reclaim their sovereignty, preserve their cultural heritage, and chart a path towards a more prosperous and self-determined future.

Debt Traps and Fiscal Irresponsibility in Africa

The challenges of debt traps and fiscal irresponsibility have plagued many African nations, hindering their economic growth and development prospects. These intertwined issues have their roots in a complex web of historical, political, and economic factors, but their consequences have been far-reaching and often detrimental to the well-being of citizens.

Debt traps refer to the vicious cycle of accumulating unsustainable levels of debt, often perpetuated by a combination of external borrowing, mismanagement of resources, and unfavorable economic conditions. Many African countries have found themselves trapped in this cycle, with debt servicing obligations consuming a significant portion of their budgets, leaving limited resources for investments in critical sectors such as education, healthcare, and infrastructure.

Fiscal irresponsibility, on the other hand, encompasses a range of practices that undermine sound financial management and economic stability. These may include excessive government spending, corruption, inefficient revenue collection systems, and a lack of accountability and transparency in public finances. Such practices not only exacerbate debt burdens but also erode public trust in institutions and undermine efforts towards sustainable development.

Breaking free from these challenges requires a concerted effort and a commitment to fiscal discipline, transparency, and responsible borrowing practices. Here are some strategies that African nations can adopt:

1. Debt Restructuring and Renegotiation

Engaging with creditors, both bilateral and multilateral, to renegotiate debt terms and explore debt relief options can provide much-needed breathing room for heavily indebted nations. This process should be accompanied by a comprehensive debt management strategy that prioritizes responsible borrowing and sustainable debt levels.

2. Diversifying Revenue Streams:

Overreliance on natural resource exports or external aid has often contributed to fiscal vulnerabilities. African nations should explore diversifying their revenue streams through the development of other economic sectors, such as manufacturing, agriculture, and services. This can reduce their susceptibility to external shocks and foster greater self-reliance.

3. Enhancing Domestic Resource Mobilization:

Strengthening tax administration systems, combating tax evasion, and broadening the tax base can bolster domestic resource mobilization efforts. These resources can then be channeled towards productive investments and social programs, reducing the need for excessive borrowing.

4. Promoting Transparency and Accountability:

Instituting robust public financial management systems, empowering oversight bodies, and fostering greater transparency in government spending can help curb corruption, mismanagement, and wasteful expenditures. This can improve public trust and ensure that resources are allocated efficiently and effectively.

5. Investing in Productive Sectors:

Rather than borrowing for consumption purposes, African nations should prioritize borrowing for investments in productive sectors that can drive economic growth and generate future revenue streams. This may include infrastructure development, human capital investments, and support for private sector development.

6. Regional Cooperation and Peer Learning:

Fostering regional cooperation and peer learning among African nations can facilitate the sharing of best practices, expertise, and resources in addressing debt challenges and promoting fiscal responsibility. Regional institutions and frameworks can play a pivotal role in this regard.

Overcoming the challenges of debt traps and fiscal irresponsibility requires a long-term commitment to sound economic policies, good governance, and a shift towards sustainable and inclusive development models. While the path may be arduous, the potential rewards of breaking free from these constraints are immense, paving the way for African nations to chart their own course towards economic prosperity and self-reliance.

The Curse of Corruption

Corruption remains a pervasive obstacle to economic development across Africa, diverting resources away from productive investments and into the pockets of corrupt officials and their cronies. From embezzlement of public funds to bribery and extortion, corruption undermines the rule of law, erodes public trust in institutions, and stifles entrepreneurship and innovation.

The looting of state coffers by corrupt leaders such as Sani Abacha in Nigeria, who embezzled billions of dollars during his time in power, leaving a legacy of economic devastation, remains a sad reminder of this notorious and cancerous decay.

Missed Opportunities for Diversification

Africa's economies remain heavily reliant on primary commodities, leaving them vulnerable to fluctuations in global prices and market demand. Despite the continent's rich diversity of resources, efforts to diversify economies and foster sustainable development have been hampered by a lack of investment, inadequate infrastructure, and a hostile business environment.

The failure of many African nations to develop value-added industries and build resilient economies capable of weathering external shocks and fostering inclusive growth.

Breaking the Chains of Mismanagement

As Africa confronts the consequences of decades of economic mismanagement, the path to redemption lies in bold reforms and visionary leadership. By promoting transparency and accountability, investing in human capital and infrastructure, and fostering a conducive environment for entrepreneurship and innovation, African nations can break free from the shackles of dependency and chart a course towards a future of shared prosperity and sustainable development.

CHAPTER 5

RELIGION AND POLITICS: A DANGEROUS TIE

THE INTERPLAY OF FAITH AND POWER

In the mosaic of Africa's socio-political landscape, the interlacing runs of religion and politics knit a complex narrative of beliefs, values, and ideologies. From the ancient rituals of indigenous spiritual traditions to the imported doctrines of Christianity, Islam, and other world religions, faith has played a central role in shaping the continent's identity and governance. Yet, amidst the rich diversity of religious expression, the bond of religion and politics has often proved to be a double-edged sword, capable of inspiring both liberation and oppression, unity and division.

The Role of Religion in African Societies

Religion occupies a central place in the lives of many Africans, providing solace, meaning, and community in the face of adversity. From the animist traditions of sub-Saharan Africa to the monotheistic faiths imported during the era of colonization, religious beliefs and practices permeate every aspect of daily life, shaping cultural norms, social structures, and moral values.

The enduring influence of traditional African religions on indigenous belief systems and cultural practices, despite centuries of missionary activity and religious conversion.

Religion as a Tool of Political Control

Throughout Africa's history, political leaders have often sought to co-opt religion as a means of legitimizing their authority and maintaining social order. From the divine right of kings to the cults of personality surrounding modern dictators, the marriage of religion and politics has been used to justify oppression, suppress dissent, and consolidate power.

The use of religious rhetoric and symbolism by authoritarian regimes to bolster their legitimacy and silence opposition, as seen in the cult of personality surrounding leaders like Mobutu Sese Seko in Zaire is a strong allusion to this point.

The Rise of Religious Extremism

In recent decades, Africa has witnessed a worrying trend towards religious extremism, fueled by a combination of political grievances, socioeconomic marginalization, and external influences. From the emergence of jihadist groups in the Sahel to the resurgence of ethno-religious violence in Nigeria and the Central African Republic, extremist ideologies have sown seeds of discord and division, threatening to tear apart the social fabric of diverse communities.

The rise of Boko Haram in Nigeria has waged a brutal campaign of violence in the name of establishing an Islamic caliphate, resulting in widespread suffering and displacement.

Toward Religious Diversity and Tolerance

Despite the challenges posed by the nexus of religion and politics, Africa remains a beacon of religious diversity and pluralism, where people of different faiths coexist harmoniously and share common bonds of humanity. By promoting interfaith dialogue, fostering religious tolerance, and upholding the principles of secularism and equality under the law, African nations can build inclusive societies that celebrate the richness of their religious heritage while safeguarding the rights and freedoms of all citizens.

Examples of countries like Senegal and Burkina Faso, where religious pluralism and tolerance are enshrined in law and practice, contributing to social cohesion and stability make this a practicable phenomenon.

Navigating the Crossroads of Faith and Governance

As Africa grapples with the complexities of religion and politics, the path forward lies in embracing the values of tolerance, pluralism, and respect for human rights. By recognizing the inherent dignity and worth of every individual, regardless of their religious affiliation, African nations can build bridges of understanding and cooperation that transcend divisions and foster unity in diversity. Only by forging a common vision of shared prosperity and mutual respect can Africa harness the transformative power of faith for the greater good of its entire people.

CHAPTER 6

THE RISE OF CABALS AND PATRONAGE NETWORKS

THE SHADOWY NETWORKS OF POWER

In the complex corridors of African governance, a web of clandestine alliances and backroom deals casts a long shadow over the aspirations of the people. Behind the façade of democracy and transparency, shadowy cabals and patronage networks wield immense influence, shaping policy decisions, monopolizing resources, and perpetuating a culture of corruption and impunity. As Africa grapples with the scourge of bad governance, the rise of these informal power structures poses a formidable challenge to the principles of accountability, justice, and equity.

Anatomy of a Cabal

At the heart of Africa's governance malaise lies the phenomenon of cabals, clandestine groups of elites who wield disproportionate influence over the levers of power. Operating outside the bounds of official institutions, these shadowy networks manipulate political processes, subvert democratic norms, and amass wealth at the expense of the public good. With tentacles extending into every sphere of society, from politics and business to media and civil society, cabals exercise a stranglehold on governance, stifling dissent and entrenching their grip on power.

The "Kitchen Cabinet" of former Nigerian President Goodluck Jonathan, a group of close advisers accused of wielding unchecked influence over government affairs is an example of such cabalism. This government continued from where the predecessors from years before stopped or rather handed over.

Patronage and Nepotism

Central to the modus operandi of cabals is the practice of patronage and nepotism, where loyalty to the ruling clique takes precedence over merit and competence. Positions of power and privilege are doled out to cronies and family members, regardless of their qualifications or suitability for the role, perpetuating a culture of cronyism and entitlement. Through the distribution of favors, contracts, and lucrative appointments, cabals ensure the loyalty of their inner circle while excluding outsiders from the corridors of influence.

The "big man" politics prevalent in many African nations, where leaders surround themselves with loyalists and relatives in key positions of authority.

Capturing the State

The capture of state institutions by cabals represents a grave threat to the principles of democracy and the rule of law. From the judiciary and law enforcement agencies to regulatory bodies and oversight mechanisms, no institution is immune from the corrosive influence of corruption and political interference. By subverting the checks and balances designed to safeguard against abuse of power, cabals undermine the integrity of governance, erode public trust in institutions, and perpetuate cycles of impunity and injustice.

The manipulation of electoral commissions and judicial systems by ruling parties to tilt the playing field in their favor, as seen in numerous African elections marred by allegations of fraud and irregularities attest to this ogre of human frailty.

Resistance and Resilience

Despite the formidable power wielded by cabals, African societies have proven resilient in the face of adversity, mobilizing grassroots movements, civil society organizations, and independent media to hold the powerful to account. From anti-corruption crusaders and investigative journalists to whistleblowers and political activists, courageous individuals across the continent have risked their lives and livelihoods to expose corruption, challenge impunity, and demand justice for the marginalized and oppressed.

The #EndSARS protests in Nigeria, where young activists mobilized to demand an end to police brutality and systemic corruption, highlighting the power of grassroots movements to effect change remains a valid but disheartening reference.

Breaking the Chains of Corruption

As Africa confronts the scourge of cabals and patronage networks, the path to liberation lies in strengthening democratic institutions, promoting transparency and accountability, and empowering citizens to reclaim their rightful place as the custodians of their own destiny.

By fostering a culture of civic engagement, nurturing independent media and civil society, and upholding the principles of justice and equality, African nations can dismantle the shadowy networks of power that have long stifled progress and prosperity. Only by shining a light into the darkest corners of governance can Africa pave the way for a future where power serves the people rather than enslaves them.

CHAPTER 7

THE PLIGHT OF THE DISENFRANCHISED

VOICES IN THE MARGINS

In the chronicles of the African societies, the voices of the disenfranchised echo in the margins, their struggles often overlooked amidst the cacophony of political intrigue and economic upheaval. From the rural subsistence farmer to the urban slum dweller, millions of Africans find themselves on the fringes of society, marginalized by systems of power and privilege that perpetuate cycles of poverty, discrimination, and exclusion.

As Africa grapples with the complexities of development and governance, the plight of the disenfranchised serves as a stark reminder of the unfinished business of liberation and the imperative of building societies where every voice is heard and every life valued.

The Faces of Marginalization

The disenfranchised entities in Africa encompass a diverse array of individuals and communities, united by their exclusion from the benefits of development and their vulnerability to exploitation and discrimination. From ethnic minorities and indigenous peoples to women, children, and persons with disabilities, marginalized groups endure the most of social and economic inequality, denied access to education, healthcare, employment, and justice.

A strong reference is the plight of the Batwa people in Uganda. This tribe faces systemic discrimination and displacement from their ancestral lands, highlighting the challenges faced by marginalized indigenous communities across Africa.

Poverty as a Form of Exclusion

At the heart of marginalization lies the scourge of poverty, which serves as both a cause and consequence of exclusion. Millions of Africans live below the poverty line, trapped in a cycle of deprivation and despair that denies them the opportunity to fulfill their potential and participate fully in society. Lacking access to basic amenities such as food, clean water, and shelter, the poor suffer marginalization not only by their material circumstances but also by the stigma and discrimination that accompany their social status.

The pervasive poverty in sub-Saharan Africa is a strong reference, Here, over 40% of the population lives on less than $1.90 a day, according to World Bank data. Yet, majority of their politicians and elite class live in super affluence in total disregard for these poor people.

The Intersections of Injustice

Marginalization in Africa is often compounded by intersecting forms of injustice, including gender inequality, ethnic discrimination, and socio-economic disparities. Women and girls, in particular, face multiple barriers to equality and empowerment, denied access to education, healthcare, and economic opportunities due to entrenched patriarchal norms and practices. Similarly, ethnic and religious minorities experience discrimination and exclusion based on their identity, perpetuating cycles of intergenerational poverty and marginalization.

The prevalence of child marriage in countries like Niger and Chad is yet an example. In these regions, girls as young as 10 are forced into marriage. This practice denies them the opportunity to pursue education and economic independence from that tender age. Eventually, most of them never recover from the bondage even in adulthood.

Empowerment through Solidarity

Despite the formidable challenges they face, the disenfranchised in Africa have demonstrated remarkable resilience and agency in their struggle for dignity and justice. From grassroots movements and civil society organizations to community-based initiatives and social enterprises, marginalized communities are mobilizing to assert their rights, demand accountability from those in power, and build inclusive societies. These give birth to environment that values and listens to every voice in every matter of life.

The work of organizations like the Women's Rights Advancement and Protection Alternative (WRAPA) in Nigeria, which advocates for the rights of women and girls and provides legal assistance to survivors of gender-based violence.*

A Call to Action

As Africa confronts the realities of marginalization and exclusion, the imperative of inclusive development has never been more urgent. By prioritizing the needs and aspirations of the disenfranchised, investing in social protection programs, and promoting policies that address the root causes of inequality and discrimination, African nations can build societies where no one is left behind. Only by standing in solidarity with the marginalized and oppressed can Africa fulfill its promise as a continent of dignity, opportunity, and hope for all its people.

CHAPTER 8

EDUCATION AS A CATALYST FOR CHANGE

THE POWER OF KNOWLEDGE

In the journey towards progress and prosperity, education stands as a beacon of hope, illuminating the path forward and empowering individuals to realize their full potential. Across Africa, the transformative power of education has the potential to break the chains of poverty, ignite the flames of innovation, and build a future where every child has the opportunity to thrive.

As Africa grapples with the complexities of development and governance, investing in education emerges as a fundamental imperative. This lays the foundation for a continent where the people cherish knowledge as the key to unlocking a brighter tomorrow.

The Promise of Education

Education is not merely a means to an end but a fundamental human right, enshrined in international conventions, regional manifestos and national constitutions as a cornerstone of democracy and development. From early childhood education to higher learning, access to quality education equips individuals with the knowledge, skills, and values necessary to navigate the complexities of the modern world, fostering critical thinking, creativity, and civic engagement.

The Universal Declaration of Human Rights is a solid reference. This charter recognizes education as a fundamental human right essential for the full realization of individual potential and the advancement of society.

Breaking the Cycle of Poverty

Education serves as a powerful tool for breaking the intergenerational cycle of poverty, offering marginalized communities a pathway to economic empowerment and social mobility. By equipping individuals with the skills and knowledge needed to secure gainful employment, education provides a means of escape from the cycle of deprivation and despair, opening doors to opportunities for self-improvement and collective prosperity.

A strong reference is the correlation between education and income levels, with each additional year of schooling associated with higher earning potential and reduced likelihood of poverty. This is according to studies by the World Bank and UNESCO.

Nurturing Global Citizens

In an increasingly interconnected world, education plays a crucial role in nurturing global citizens who are equipped to navigate the complexities of multiculturalism, diversity, and globalization. By promoting intercultural understanding, tolerance, and empathy, education fosters the values of peace, social cohesion, and sustainable development, laying the groundwork for a more inclusive and equitable society.

We can refer to the UNESCO Global Citizenship Education initiative, which aims to equip learners with the knowledge, skills, and attitudes needed to contribute to a more just, peaceful, and sustainable world.

Overcoming Barriers to Access

Despite the transformative potential of education, millions of children across Africa continue to be denied access to quality learning opportunities due to systemic barriers such as poverty, gender inequality, armed conflict, and lack of infrastructure. Addressing these barriers requires a multi-faceted approach that includes targeted interventions such as school feeding programs, scholarships for marginalized groups, and investments in teacher training and educational infrastructure.

The UNESCO Education for All initiative, which aims to ensure that all children, regardless of their circumstances, have access to quality education by 2030 is a pointer to the importance of education in this respect.

The Imperative of Investment

As Africa confronts the challenges of the 21st century, the imperative of investment in education has never been more urgent. By prioritizing education as a fundamental human right and a driver of sustainable development, African nations can unlock the potential of their people, unleash the forces of innovation and creativity, and build a future where every child has the opportunity to learn, grow, and thrive. Only by investing in education can Africa realize its vision of a continent where knowledge is cherished as the key to unlocking a brighter tomorrow for generations to come.

CHAPTER 9

HARNESSING TECHNOLOGY FOR DEVELOPMENT

THE DIGITAL FRONTIER

In the digital age, technology stands as a potent force for change, reshaping the contours of society and revolutionizing the way we live, work, and interact. Across Africa, the transformative power of technology has the potential to bridge the gap between aspiration and achievement, unlocking new opportunities for economic empowerment, social inclusion, and sustainable development. As Africa navigates the complexities of the 21st century, harnessing technology emerges as a fundamental imperative, paving the way for a continent where innovation thrives, and progress knows no bounds.

The Promise of Digital Innovation

Technology holds the promise of leapfrogging traditional barriers to development, offering African nations a pathway to leapfrog into the digital age and overcome longstanding challenges such as limited access to infrastructure, healthcare, education, and financial services.

From mobile banking and e-commerce to telemedicine and distance learning, digital innovation has the potential to revolutionize the delivery of essential services, improve livelihoods, and empower communities to chart their own course towards prosperity.

The proliferation of mobile phone technology in Africa has transformed the continent's communication landscape and opened up new opportunities for economic and social development.

Bridging the Digital Divide

Despite the promise of digital innovation, Africa continues to grapple with the digital divide, with significant disparities in access to technology and internet connectivity between urban and rural areas, as well as between rich and poor communities.

Addressing this digital divide requires concerted efforts to expand access to affordable broadband infrastructure, promote digital literacy and skills development, and ensure that marginalized groups have equal opportunities to participate in the digital economy.

The World Bank's Digital Economy for Africa initiative seeks to expand broadband connectivity and digital skills training across the continent to bridge the digital divide and unlock the potential of Africa's digital economy.

Technology for Social Impact

In addition to driving economic growth, technology has the potential to address some of Africa's most pressing social and environmental challenges, from healthcare and education to agriculture and environmental conservation. By harnessing the power of data analytics, artificial intelligence, and machine learning, African innovators are developing solutions that improve healthcare delivery, enhance agricultural productivity, and promote environmental sustainability, leading to tangible improvements in the quality of life for millions of people.

The use of mobile health (mHealth) applications in Africa to provide access to healthcare services in remote and underserved areas. However, this improves health outcomes and reduces healthcare disparities.

Fostering a Culture of Innovation

Realizing the potential of technology for development requires more than just access to digital infrastructure; it also requires nurturing a culture of innovation and entrepreneurship that fosters creativity, risk-taking, and collaboration. Governments, academia, and the private sector must work together to create an enabling environment for innovation, providing support for startups, research and development initiatives, and technology hubs that serve as incubators for new ideas and solutions.

The rise of tech hubs and innovation ecosystems across Africa, from Nairobi's Silicon Savannah to Cape Town's Silicon Cape are driving entrepreneurship and technological innovation across the continent.

Embracing the Digital Future

As Africa stands on the brink of a digital revolution, the imperative of harnessing technology for development has never been more urgent. By investing in digital infrastructure, promoting digital literacy and skills development, and fostering a culture of innovation and entrepreneurship, African nations can unlock the transformative potential of technology and build a future where progress knows no bounds. Only by embracing the digital future can Africa seize the opportunities of the 21st century and realize its vision of a continent where innovation thrives, and prosperity is shared by all.

CHAPTER 10

TOWARDS SUSTAINABLE DEVELOPMENT

EXPEDITING ACTION

In the crucible of the 21st century, Africa stands at a crossroads, poised on the threshold of unprecedented opportunity and daunting challenges. As the continent grapples with the complexities of development and governance, the imperative of sustainable development emerges as a fundamental imperative. This provides guidance on the path towards a future where prosperity is shared equitably, and the planet is safeguarded for future generations. In the pursuit of sustainable development, Africa has the potential to not only transform its own destiny but also to chart a course towards a more just, inclusive, and sustainable world.

Understanding Sustainable Development

Sustainable development is more than just a buzzword; it is a holistic approach to development that seeks to balance economic growth, social inclusion, and environmental protection, ensuring that the needs of present generations are met without compromising the ability of future generations to meet their own needs.

By integrating economic, social, and environmental considerations into decision-making processes, sustainable development offers a blueprint for building resilient, inclusive, and equitable societies.

The United Nations Sustainable Development Goals (SDGs), a universal call to action, is a strong reference. This clarion call is to end poverty, protect the planet, and ensure that all people enjoy peace and prosperity by 2030.

The Triple Bottom Line: People, Planet, Prosperity

At the heart of sustainable development lies the concept of the triple bottom line, which emphasizes the interconnectedness of economic, social, and environmental outcomes. By promoting inclusive economic growth, investing in human capital, and protecting natural resources and ecosystems, African nations can create a virtuous cycle of prosperity that lifts people out of poverty, strengthens communities, and preserves the planet for future generations.

Reference: The African Union's Agenda 2063, which envisions a prosperous, integrated, and peaceful Africa driven by its own citizens and representing a dynamic force in the global arena.

Building Resilient Communities

Sustainable development is about more than just numbers on a balance sheet; it is about building resilient communities that can withstand shocks and adapt to changing circumstances. By investing in social protection systems, disaster preparedness, and climate resilience measures, African nations can empower communities to weather the storms of economic uncertainty, environmental degradation, and social upheaval, ensuring that no one is left behind in the pursuit of progress.

The role of community-based organizations and grassroots movements in driving sustainable development at the local level. From women's cooperatives promoting sustainable agriculture to youth-led initiatives advocating for climate action, all these are for the development of African rural and urban entities into mega cities.

Partnerships for Progress

Achieving sustainable development requires collaborative action across sectors and stakeholders, from governments and civil society to the private sector and international organizations. By forging partnerships for progress, African nations can leverage the expertise, resources, and innovative solutions needed to tackle complex challenges such as poverty, inequality, and climate change, mobilizing collective action towards a shared vision of a better future for all.

The Addis Ababa Action Agenda, which calls for strengthened international cooperation and partnership to support African countries in their efforts to achieve sustainable development.

A Vision for Tomorrow

As Africa embarks on the journey towards sustainable development, the path ahead is fraught with challenges and opportunities. By embracing the principles of sustainability, equity, and resilience, African nations can overcome adversity, unleash the potential of their people, and build a future where prosperity is shared equitably, and the planet is preserved for generations to come. Only by working together in solidarity and unity of purpose can Africa realize its vision of a continent where sustainable development is not just a distant dream but a lived reality for all its people.

CHAPTER 11

CULTIVATING GOOD GOVERNANCE

THE FOUNDATION OF PROGRESS

At the heart of Africa's journey towards prosperity lies the imperative of good governance – a system of accountable, transparent, and inclusive governance that serves the interests of the people and upholds the rule of law. As Africa confronts the complexities of development and governance, cultivating good governance emerges as a fundamental imperative, providing the bedrock upon which progress, stability, and prosperity can be built. In the pursuit of good governance, Africa has the potential to unlock the transformative power of democracy, justice, and integrity, paving the way for a future where the aspirations of its people are realized, and the promise of the continent is fulfilled.

The Pillars of Good Governance

Several key pillars, including democracy, rule of law, accountability, transparency, and participation, characterize good governance. By upholding these principles, governments can ensure that it exercises power responsibly, make decisions in the public interest, and empower citizens to hold their leaders to account. From free and fair elections to independent judiciaries and vibrant civil societies, these pillars provide the scaffolding upon which good governance rests.

The African Charter on Democracy, Elections and Governance, which affirms the commitment of African nations to the principles of democracy, rule of law, and respect for human rights.

Strengthening Democratic Institutions

Central to the project of good governance is the strengthening of democratic institutions, including legislatures, judiciaries, electoral commissions, and anti-corruption agencies. By ensuring the separation of powers, checks and balances, and mechanisms for citizen engagement, democratic institutions can serve as bulwarks against abuse of power, corruption, and authoritarianism, safeguarding the rights and freedoms of all citizens.

The role of independent electoral commissions in ensuring the integrity and credibility of elections remains an inspirational guide and strong reference. We have seen this in Ghana and South Africa, where the successful transition to democracy have taken place.

Promoting Transparency and Accountability

Transparency and accountability are essential cornerstones of good governance, providing mechanisms for citizens to access information, scrutinize government actions, and hold leaders to account for their decisions and actions. By enacting freedom of information laws, strengthening oversight mechanisms, and promoting civic engagement and participation, governments can foster a culture of openness, responsiveness, and trust that enhances the legitimacy and effectiveness of governance.

The Open Government Partnership (OGP), a global initiative that brings together governments and civil society organizations to promote transparency, citizen participation, and accountability.

Combatting Corruption

Corruption remains a pervasive obstacle to good governance across Africa, undermining trust in institutions, eroding public confidence, and diverting resources away from essential services and development priorities. By enacting and enforcing robust anti-corruption laws, strengthening investigative and prosecutorial capacities, and promoting a culture of integrity and ethics, governments can root out corruption at all levels and build systems of governance that are accountable, transparent, and responsive to the needs of the people.

The work of anti-corruption agencies such as Nigeria's Economic and Financial Crimes Commission (EFCC) and Kenya's Ethics and Anti-Corruption Commission (EACC) in investigating and prosecuting cases of corruption and promoting accountability and transparency in governance.

A Call to Leadership

As Africa charts its course towards a future of prosperity and progress, the imperative of cultivating good governance has never been more urgent. By upholding the principles of democracy, rule of law, transparency, and accountability, African nations can build systems of governance that empower citizens, promote justice and equality, and ensure that the promise of the continent is fulfilled for generations to come.

Only by embracing the ideals of good governance can Africa realize its vision of a continent where the aspirations of its people are realized, and the promise of a brighter tomorrow is within reach.

CHAPTER 12

Fostering Regional Integration and Cooperation

THE POWER OF UNITY

In the mixture of African diversity, the vision of unity and integration shines as a beacon of hope, illuminating the path towards a future of peace, prosperity, and progress. As Africa confronts the complexities of development and governance, fostering regional integration and cooperation emerges as a fundamental imperative, transcending borders and divisions to harness the collective strength and potential of the continent. In the pursuit of regional integration, Africa has the potential to overcome historical legacies of division and conflict, build resilient economies, and forge a common destiny rooted in solidarity and mutual respect.

The Imperative of Regional Integration

Regional integration is essential to unlocking the full potential of Africa's economies and societies, promoting trade, investment, and collaboration across borders. By breaking down barriers to movement of goods, services, and people, regional integration can foster economic diversification, stimulate growth, and create jobs, lifting millions out of poverty and driving sustainable development.

The African Continental Free Trade Area (AfCFTA), a landmark agreement that seeks to create a single market for goods and services in Africa, with the potential to boost intra-African trade by up to 52% by 2022, according to the United Nations Economic Commission for Africa (UNECA).

Strengthening Regional Institutions

Central to the project of regional integration is the strengthening of regional institutions and mechanisms for cooperation, coordination, and conflict resolution. From regional economic communities such as the Economic Community of West African States (ECOWAS) and the Southern African Development Community (SADC) to continental bodies like the African Union (AU), these institutions play a crucial role in promoting peace, stability, and development across Africa.

The role of regional organizations in mediating conflicts, facilitating peacekeeping operations, and promoting dialogue and reconciliation, as seen in the efforts of ECOWAS to resolve the political crisis in The Gambia in 2017.

Promoting Infrastructure Development

Infrastructure development is a key enabler of regional integration, connecting countries and regions through networks of roads, railways, ports, and energy infrastructure. By investing in cross-border infrastructure projects, African nations can reduce trade costs, enhance connectivity, and unlock the potential of regional markets, laying the foundation for inclusive growth and sustainable development.

The Trans-African Highways Network and the Programme for Infrastructure Development in Africa (PIDA), initiatives aimed at improving transportation infrastructure and connectivity across the continent.

Fostering People-to-People Ties

Beyond the realm of economics and politics, regional integration is also about building bridges of understanding and cooperation among the people of Africa. By promoting cultural exchange, educational partnerships, and people-to-people ties, African nations can nurture a sense of solidarity and common identity that transcends national borders, fostering mutual respect and appreciation for the rich diversity of African heritage and culture.

The African Union's Agenda 2063, which emphasizes the importance of promoting cultural exchange and collaboration among African nations as a means of fostering unity and solidarity.

A Continent United

As Africa strides boldly into the future, the imperative of fostering regional integration and cooperation has never been more urgent. By embracing the ideals of unity, solidarity, and mutual respect, African nations can overcome the challenges of the past and forge a common destiny rooted in peace, prosperity, and progress. Only by working together in solidarity and partnership can Africa realize its vision of a continent where the aspirations of its people are realized, and the promise of a brighter tomorrow is within reach.

CONCLUSION

Embracing Africa's Destiny

As we come to the close of this exploration into the multifaceted challenges facing Africa, it becomes clear that the continent stands at a pivotal moment in its history. From the shadows of colonial exploitation to the complexities of contemporary governance, Africa has navigated a tumultuous journey marked by triumphs and setbacks, progress and stagnation. Yet, amidst the trials and tribulations, one truth emerges with undeniable clarity: Africa's destiny lies not in the hands of fate, but in the collective will and determination of its people.

Throughout this book, we have explored the depths of Africa's economic, political, social, and cultural landscape, uncovering the root causes of its most pressing challenges and exploring pathways towards sustainable solutions. We have confronted the specter of corruption and mismanagement, grappled with the nexus of religion and politics, and championed the cause of marginalized communities and disenfranchised voices. We have celebrated the transformative power of education and technology, and championed the virtues of good governance and regional integration.

Yet, as we reflect on the complexities of Africa's journey, we are reminded that the road ahead is fraught with uncertainty and adversity. The challenges facing Africa are formidable, from entrenched poverty and inequality to environmental degradation and political instability. Yet, in the face of these challenges, we are also reminded of the resilience, ingenuity, and boundless potential of the African spirit.

Final Strokes

In the final analysis, the future of Africa lies not in the hands of external actors or forces beyond its control, but in the hands of its own people. It is the young entrepreneur harnessing the power of technology to drive innovation and create jobs. It is the grassroots activist fighting for justice and equality in the face of oppression. It is the visionary leader charting a course towards a brighter future for generations to come.

As we turn the final page of this book, let us do so with a renewed sense of hope and purpose. Let us embrace Africa's destiny with courage, conviction, and determination. Let us stand united in our commitment to building a continent where prosperity is shared equitably, justice is upheld without compromise, and the promise of Africa is fulfilled for its entire people.

For in the end, it is not the challenges we face that define us, but how we rise to meet them. And in the journey towards Africa's collective destiny, let us rise together, as one continent, one people, bound by the shared dream of a better tomorrow.

The story of Africa is still being written, and the final chapter has yet to be written. Nevertheless, as we embark on the next chapter of Africa's journey, let us do so with unwavering faith in the power of the African spirit to overcome, to innovate, and to flourish. For Africa's destiny is not a destination, but a journey – and the best is yet to come.